To Greg:

Best wishes for your continued success.

Randy Kidd

`D1261175`

the
Myths &
Methods
of being a
Manager

the Myths & Methods of being a Manager

Kandy Kidd

Illustrated by Georgia Pana
Cover design by Scott Wolff

Brendon Hill Publishing Co.

Published by:
Brendon Hill Publishing Co.
6116 Merced Avenue Suite 192
Oakland, Ca 94611
(415) 895-7033

Printed in the United States of America

Library of Congress Cataloging in Publication Data

Kidd, Kandy, 1954-
  The myths & methods of being a manager.

  Bibliography: p.
  1. Executive ability. 2. Management. I. Title.
II. Title: Myths and methods of being a manager.
HD38.2.K53   1986   658.4'09   86-70806
ISBN 0-937751-31-6

DEDICATION

To my husband, Bill, whose attention to
detail is my saving grace

To my parents, Ginger and Tom, who gave
me a unique name and the desire to
make something of it

To my sisters, Gail, Barbara, Nancy and
Karen, who gave me dormitory living
long before college

ACKNOWLEDGMENTS

I would like to publicly thank the following individuals who contributed their ideas, talent, and moral support to this book:

Ross Bell, Robert Beller, Jason Bishop, Dan Boyle, Dave Carey, Vicki DeRosa, Loralie Froman, Anthony Fuschillo, Joyce Gray, Eric Harvey, Karen and Fred Honold, Elma and Marlin Hurd, Jeffrey Kreis, Bill McGrane, Lowell Moss, Georgia Pana, Kathy Rivera, Lew Russell, Carey Westall, Scott Wolff.

Special thanks to Debbie Chapman, Carol Kinsey Goman, Gary Hickox, and Judy McGowan for the countless hours they devoted to this effort.

I also want to express a loving thank you to my husband, Bill, who has been a constant source of inspiration and a continuous sounding board for ideas. Finally, heartfelt thanks to my family for their love and support and for knowing how I wish Dad could have shared this.

CONTENTS

Chapter 1:
Do You Know
These People?

"Briggs...Crane...Congratulations. I'm promoting you both to manage two of my most important departments."

"Both departments are overworked, understaffed, over budget, behind schedule and morale is at an all time low."

"So, Briggs...Crane...Good Luck. And, by the way, the people in these departments really resent your promotions."

"Are we having fun yet?"

David Briggs and Susan Crane are about to embark on an incredible journey through time and space. During this journey, they will encounter endless challenges from numerous life forms, experience excruciating pain in the form of long meetings and suffer hair-raising terror from screaming to-do lists. No, they are not entering the Twilight Zone—they are taking the first step into management positions with supervisory responsibility.

David and Susan have earned these promotions through demonstrated competence in previous non-supervisory assignments. Like many managers, however, David and Susan have had no training in people management. As a result, their promotions can turn into nightmares—either for them or, most likely, for the people they will manage.

Management myth #1:

*Managerial skills
are located
on the 19th pair
of chromosomes.*

To date, science has failed to isolate the chromosome that determines a manager's effectiveness in getting things done through others. Therefore, due to the growing belief that people skills are learned rather than inherited, this book has been developed as a practical alternative to genetic modeling.

For the new manager, this book refutes prevailing management myths and provides a comprehensive how-to guide for developing interpersonal skills. For the experienced manager, it is a refresher that offers an objective look at skills already in use. For the mentor, it serves as a useful resource in preparing protégés for their first step into supervisory management.

This guide book is not an exercise in theory. Quite the opposite—it illustrates specific techniques that can improve team performance by building employee trust and commitment. Not only does this book include practical suggestions for managing others, it also identifies the common managerial pitfalls to avoid. This book offers a collection of tools that have been successful in numerous situations, but does not claim itself as the sole solution to every managerial problem. Rather, you can evaluate the applicability of each tool and choose whether to incorporate these ideas into your own management behavior. A Reader's Notes section is available at the back of the book for recording your thoughts on how these concepts can be applied to your management role.

Finally, the content is both informative and entertaining, designed to facilitate greater learning.

Humor is an effective stress reliever and allows us to view situations from the proper perspective. This book offers humorous glimpses of everyday situations and reminds managers not to take themselves too seriously. Remember, if you can laugh at yourself, you will never cease to be amused.

Chapter 2:
Are Your Strengths
Working Against You?

"I think one of my strengths as a manager is the ability to analyze situations."

"Yeah, but you have to be careful that you don't over-analyze and read too much into things."

"Good morning Crane. Good morning Briggs."

"Now what do you suppose he means by that remark?"

In the biographies of successful managers, self-knowledge of personal strengths and weaknesses is a common theme. In fact, truly successful individuals refer to weaknesses as "potential growth areas" because they believe personal and professional development is an ongoing process.

Everyone has strengths and potential growth areas, and a first step in self-understanding is to identify your own characteristics within these two categories. Start by dividing a blank page in the Reader's Notes section into two columns and listing the personal characteristics which represent strengths. To develop your list of strengths, consider work situations you handled very successfully and describe the skills used and how you behaved. Then think of work situations you handled less effectively and repeat the process to identify potential growth areas.

Once you have identified your particular strengths, you can then maximize these strengths, right? Well . . . sort of.

Management myth #2:

*You can never
have too much of
a good thing.*

The irony of this myth is that the individuals who espouse it are often described by others as "coming on too strong." A strength, if overextended, can work against you. In other words, the very skill or behavior that represents a professional quality can reduce your managerial effectiveness if it is overused. The following examples illustrate some common overuses of managerial strengths:

1. Self-confidence is regarded as a strength because, generally, the more confident people feel, the better they perform. But if a manager is overly confident and fails to consult with or heed advice from others, team effectiveness will suffer.

2. Analytical skill represents a positive attribute because managers must effectively identify and solve problems. But if a manager uses a high level of analysis for even the smallest problems, the resulting paperwork can become a bigger obstacle than the original problem.

3. The empathetic manager is sensitive to employee concerns and offers personal assistance to others. But if the manager is overly supportive, the tendency to rescue employees rather than helping them to help themselves is detrimental to employee development.

4. Accuracy is a positive characteristic which allows managers to maintain high-quality work standards. But if meticulous preparation turns into perfectionism, the manager causes unnecessary delays and becomes intolerant of mistakes.

5. Optimism is a desirable trait because a positive outlook builds enthusiasm and helps a manager to view problems as opportunities. But if excessive optimism creates a Pollyanna, the manager will be unrealistic in sizing-up situations.

6. The innovative manager is highly regarded since organizations must stay on the leading edge of change in order to excel. But if innovation becomes nothing more than change for the sake of change, insufficient planning can hurt the organization.

We all know individuals who exhibit these tendencies. Thus, when maximizing strengths, consider the risk of overextending those strengths. To do so, review the positive side of your own list and ask how an overuse of traits could work against you or may have worked against you in past situations. Develop your strengths by knowing their limitations.

To gain more objective input, show your list to two associates who work closely with you and ask them for feedback. This can be very enlightening in terms of understanding how others see you.

For even greater objectivity, consider a self-assessment instrument, a questionnaire which asks you to make a series of choices about your inter-personal characteristics. It is called an instrument instead of a test because there are no right or wrong answers. Based on your responses, the instrument provides a description of predominant behavioral tendencies.

Due to the vast interest in self-improvement, personal growth seminars offering instrument-based learning are readily available. Information on how to select a self-assessment instrument is included in the Appendix.

After taking the instrument according to how you see yourself, you can gain further insight from your associates by asking them to take the instrument according to how *they* see you. The results will identify your behavioral tendencies most visible to others.

These suggestions represent a significant first step toward developing an understanding of your interpersonal characteristics. To manage others effectively, you must first know yourself—insight out.

Chapter 3:
Do You Use or Choose
Your Management Style?

"I can't decide which management style I want to use."

"Doesn't it depend on the situation you're dealing with?"

"I guess so . . . maybe I should decide not to decide."

"Maybe so . . . indecision: the choice of a new generation."

Initial studies on management style erroneously presumed that all successful managers possessed a single set of positive traits. Had this "great person" concept been correct, these researchers could have teamed up with the chromosome researchers (Chapter 1) to manufacture effective managers by the thousands. However, for every leadership trait you can think of, a successful leader without that trait can be cited.

People are not successful simply because they have a certain management style. No one style is effective 100% of the time. The examples that follow focus on three of the many different styles of management:

1. The directive style uses authority and tells others what to do.
2. The supportive style offers assistance and relates to others.
3. The analytical style gathers data and goes through a high level of problem-solving.

Now, suppose your team suffers a temporary setback which shakes the group's confidence. Which style is most effective? Directive? Not really. When the team is down, barking out orders adds to the group's tension and does little to build self-esteem. The most effective approach is to rebuild team confidence through a supportive style.

Next, assume that your group faces a crisis situation with a critically short deadline. Which style do you use? Analytical? No. This is not the time to develop a detailed business case. The most effective approach is to issue clear assignments for immediate action through a directive style. (NOTE: You must first earn your people's trust, however, if you want them to do it your way without question.)

And which style do you employ when your group is selected to move the organization into uncharted waters? Supportive? No. All the stroking in the world is not as productive as the strategic planning approach of the analytical style.

Looks like simple common sense, doesn't it?

Management myth #3:

*Common sense
is common
practice.*

Unfortunately, most managers tend to use the one style that feels most natural to them regardless of the situation. Managers who are most comfortable with the directive style, for example, tend to be directive the majority of the time. As a result, they reduce their effectiveness when this style is applied to the wrong situation.

No single style is appropriate for all employees, in all situations, at all times. Therefore, consciously avoiding the trap of employing the one style you are most comfortable with can increase your management effectiveness. Do not eliminate your present style; rather, increase your versatility by adding to your behavioral repertoire. Successful managers are those individuals who choose the appropriate behavior for each situation they are in and each individual with whom they interact.

Some managers resist this approach because they see it as catering to their employees. But if adaptability is viewed as a powerful managerial skill, you can interact with team members in a way that maximizes each individual's potential. Bear Bryant, one of the most successful college football coaches, was quoted as saying: "I don't treat everybody alike; everybody is different. But I do treat everybody fair."[1]

In other words, managers should recognize the fact that each person has a distinctive way of thinking, feeling and acting which represents an individual perspective. This perspective, in turn, governs the way people relate to and perform in various situations. Managers who use the same approach with all people incorrectly assume that everyone shares the same perspective. For example, will a logical, detail-oriented team member react positively to a creative, abstract approach? No. The team member will probably become defensive rather than concentrating on getting the job done. But if the management style is more precise and systematic, the communication will be productive. In a similar vein, managers who avoid taking risks should adapt their style when interacting with innovative, change-oriented team members. In other words, if the manager is only interested in minimizing risk, communication is likely to be strained and creativity stifled.

Have you ever seen a picture in which multiple images are present? You may see one image while the person next to you sees something else. Even after the other images are pointed out you may still have some difficulty in seeing them. With a little practice, however, you can comfortably move back and forth between the images. Flexibility in management works in much the same manner. At first, you may experience difficulty in understanding another team member's perspective; but with practice you can learn to consider other perspectives and adapt your management style to facilitate communication.

This analogy of the multiple image picture also applies to conflict, since conflict results when different mindsets come together. Difficulty in getting along with someone is often caused by dissimilar views of a situation. If you can openly address differing points of view rather than disregarding them, you will more effectively manage conflict.

Another challenge for managers is learning to appreciate the unique contributions these individual differences represent. Organizations need a healthy mix of styles and usually benefit from diverse points of view. Conflicting mindsets often lead to new ideas. In her book, *The Change Masters*, Rosabeth Moss Kanter states that "innovation flourishes . . . (when) differences are recognized and even encouraged." Therefore, rather than molding others in their own image or staffing their organizations with carbon copies of themselves, managers have far more to gain by adapting their style to encompass the team's individual mindsets.

By understanding and respecting individual differences, the manager can become more productive in everyday communication. While functional and technical skills played a major role in your initial promotion to supervisory management, adaptive skills will contribute most strongly to long-term success in managing others.

Chapter 4:
Do You Listen With Your Mouth Open?

"...which is why the situation is quite serious——"

"Briggs, let me interrupt for just a moment."

"I agree that your problem is serious. . ."

". . . it's just not very interesting."

Listening is a management skill that is often underdeveloped. As a matter of fact, some managers do not think of listening as a skill at all; they accept the "lousy listener" label because, until very recently, training to increase listening skills had not been emphasized.

Madelyn Burley Allen, author of *Listening: The Forgotten Skill*, states that "the school system has accepted the myth that we were born knowing how to listen." She supports this statement by identifying the years of formal training people receive in each communication mode:

Writing	12 years
Reading	6-8 years
Speaking	1-2 years
Listening	0-1/2 years

As you can see, the major emphasis is on writing. Yet, what portion of a manager's daily communication is spent writing? Dr. Paul Rankin of Ohio State University monitored the activities of 65 managers for a two month period and found that they spent 70% of their day in communication.[2] More specifically, the breakdown of their communication was:

Writing	9 percent
Reading	16 percent
Speaking	35 percent
Listening	40 percent

This study suggests that managers spend the most time utilizing their least developed mode of communication. Think about the time you spend listening during a day's telephone calls. You could be earning over a third of your salary for this function alone.

Yet there is one more listening statistic that is particularly alarming. Dr. Harry Jones at Columbia University tested the listening comprehension of students immediately following a ten minute talk. To his surprise, the students could correctly answer only 50% of the test items. Two months later, comprehension dropped to 25%.[3] These same results were obtained by Dr. Ralph G. Nichols at the University of Minnesota, who reduced the retest period to two weeks.[4] Studies were also conducted at Florida State, Michigan State and Denver University with the same conclusion: people operate at a 25% listening efficiency. When you multiply the amount of time you spend listening by .25, it equates to a huge loss in productivity.

Think back to your reaction in school when pop-quizzes were given. Typically, you did not do as well on the first quiz as you did on the next quiz. Why? The knowledge that you might be quizzed at any time caused you to listen more carefully. As a result, you learned more and did better on subsequent quizzes. This suggests that, for most people, listening inefficiency is not caused by an inherent lack of skill— it is caused by a failure to develop an ability you already possess.

Management myth #4:

Speaking is
more powerful
than listening.

The commanding speaker usually conjures a more powerful mental image than the effective listener. Most meetings are characterized by people queuing up to express their point of view without listening to what was said before them or after them. Few managers view meetings as an opportunity to listen. Yet listening is a very powerful communication skill. Successful salespeople claim that they listen their way into more sales than they talk their way into; by listening to the prospect's needs, the sales approach can then be tailored to meet those needs.

Listening is also a strong negotiation skill. Jeffrey Kreis, owner of three highly successful California restaurants, accidentally experienced the power of listening at a major negotiation meeting which concerned the construction of two new restaurants.[5] A day before the meeting, Jeffrey developed laryngitis, but he could not cancel the meeting due to the developer's busy schedule. Jeffrey was apprehensive about not being able to talk, so he prepared an agenda listing the items he considered negotiable.

During the meeting, Jeffrey could only point to the various items and open them up for everyone else's discussion. To his amazement, he walked away from that meeting with the developer's agreement to provide every item on the list. Based on the outcomes of previous negotiation meetings where Jeffrey had been very vocal, he is convinced that his listening posture significantly increased his effectiveness.

Once you recognize the value and power behind listening, you can immediately begin developing this skill:

1. Concentrate on what is being said. The human brain can think three times faster than the average person speaks. As a matter of fact, cassette players are now available that double the tape speed so that managers can listen to a one hour voice recording in just 30 minutes. During daily conversations, however, managers often use this extra brain capacity to think about other things while they are supposed to be listening. Some managers have become so adept at faking attention that they actually appear to be listening (through eye contact and nodding), though their mind is reviewing tomorrow's meeting with the VP. When the employee stops talking, the classic non-listening response is to ask the employee to "send me a memo on that so I can give it further consideration." The exchange is a waste of time for both parties, since the memo will probably require another face-to-face discussion. Instead, if you use total brain capacity to think about what is being said, comprehension is increased.

2. Listen first, then respond. Many managers create misunderstandings by concentrating on what they will say next rather than listening. As a result, these managers end up hearing only what they want to hear or they respond with apples when the employee is talking about oranges. Even worse, when information does not make sense, the mind automatically fills in the blanks. Anyone who has witnessed the rumor chain game has observed this process, in which the original message gets so distorted that the end product bears little or no resemblance.

Through active listening, you can address the correct issue and let the speaker know you have understood the message. Sometimes, before responding, you may want to paraphrase what has been said. This is particularly helpful before you agree to something or before you disagree. Many arguments begin when two individuals focus on different points, or when they actually agree without realizing it because neither of them is listening. At the very least, paraphrasing will help you clarify what you disagree about. Also, by briefly restating instructions or directions, you reduce the likelihood of crossed wires.

3. Try to avoid defensive responses. When managers become defensive, they stop listening as they mentally prepare a rebuttal. For example, if an employee complains about continually receiving the difficult assignments, many managers defensively respond by saying, "All work is equally distributed," and a disagreement is likely to ensue. But if you maintain your objectivity and paraphrase what you heard by saying, "It sounds like you think I'm unfair about the way I distribute work," you can diffuse the employee's resistance and more calmly discuss the problem. (NOTE: You are not agreeing with the employee, you are merely demonstrating that you are listening.) It is difficult for people to remain angry when you listen to them. Try it.

4. Bring your listening skills to lectures and presentations. Many times we label a presentation in advance, supposing it will be too complex or too boring, or that nothing new will be introduced. However, if you adopt a positive attitude by saying, "If I can get one helpful idea, it will be worthwhile," you are more likely to take something useful away with you.

Also, note-taking should focus on ideas rather than details. Managers who concentrate more on note-taking than on listening usually miss the message. Instead, jot down key phrases or main points that will reinforce your comprehension of what was said.

Try to resist distractions such as doodling. Sit where you can see and hear, and consciously decide not to let noises interfere with your listening. It is possible to hear noises without being distracted by them. If the speaker has annoying mannerisms, focus on content rather than delivery and listening will be much more effective.

5. Take a listening course. Seminars are available which develop listening abilities. If possible, choose one that includes a listening profile (self-assessment questionnaire) to help pinpoint your listening behavior and provide specific suggestions to increase listening efficiency.

Listening is an important management skill and one which you can develop quickly. When you make an effort to listen, your ears become valuable resources for acquiring the ideas and information needed for success.

Chapter 5:
Is Time On Your Side or Your Back?

"I never seem to have enough time, Dave. There simply aren't enough hours in the day."

"I feel the same way. Sometimes I wish I could just stop the clock to get caught up . . . . but"

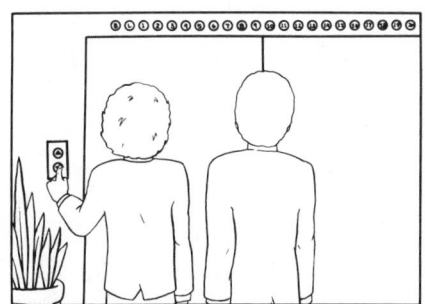

"time always disappears when I need it the most."

"Yeah, kind of like Adams on a Friday afternoon."

Time management has become one of the hottest buzz words around the workplace, yet it is usually accompanied by the quip, "Sure, it's important—but who's got the time?"

Management myth #5:

*The real secret
to time management
is working faster
and staying later.*

Many managers unknowingly subscribe to this myth, believing there is no other way of staying on top of their job. Yet a study of 2,443 managers conducted by industrial psychologists Allen I. Kraut and Andrea S. Goldberg found no correlation between effectiveness ratings and the amount of time worked.[6] While late hours are usually required for special projects and emergencies, they are no guarantee of increased performance. And working faster leaves less time for thinking and more room for error.

Numerous time management courses are available which provide specific formats for increasing organizational skills, by using calendars, desk organizers, call records and filing systems. Before taking a course, however, it is helpful to pinpoint time wasters and consider the following suggestions for reducing them:

1. Determine where your time goes. Have you ever looked at the clock to discover the workday was over? Many managers lose track of time because of the numerous activities they are involved in each day. Therefore, an excellent starting point in managing time is to understand how you are currently spending it. For the next two days, keep a time log recording your activity each hour. You may be surprised to learn that the biggest time consumers have the least to do with your management role.

2. Sort your paperwork. Color coded folders are excellent tools for sorting paperwork into categories that make sense for you. Instead of shuffling paperwork, build the habit of taking action on each piece of paper you touch. For example, place material

that requires action in a red folder, memos or letters that provide information in a yellow folder, and put reading material such as trade journals and reports in a blue folder. Depending on your responsibilities, you may also have a signature folder or a project update folder. The point is to develop a system that works for you by organizing your paperwork around appropriate priorities.

3. Consolidate your activities. Once your paperwork is sorted, concentrate on one type of activity at a time. If you begin with the red folder (action), make sure to take action on each piece of paper, such as delegating a task, writing a response, or requesting more information. In a similar manner, try to return all your telephone calls at the same time. As a result, you will save time that was previously spent shifting from one activity to another.

Next, determine the best time to handle the yellow folder which contains information you must read that day. As you go through this folder, use the waste-basket liberally. Over 80% of items filed are never retrieved, so be certain you need the information before filing it. For those items you are unsure of, label a folder with a question mark and date every document that goes into it. Then, once a month, purge this file of any information that is 90 days old or more.

Lastly, by placing the blue folder (reading) in your briefcase, you are prepared to use unexpected free time, such as late appointments and meeting delays, more productively. This practice allows you to use waiting time during business travel to keep current on your trade journals.

4. Use the telephone wisely. Recognize its potential as both a timesaver and time waster. Use it to confirm appointments and clarify instructions. State or discern the purpose of a call as quickly as possible to avoid unnecessarily long telephone conversations. Also, when decisions can be made by telephone rather than in a face-to-face meeting, you will save valuable travel time.

5. Distribute and request meeting agendas. Often, the reasons for holding meetings are unclear, the same issues recur, and nothing seems to get accomplished. In developing an agenda, make sure meeting issues are clearly stated and are relevant. Also, by requesting agendas from others, you can avoid wasting everyone's time in a poorly planned meeting or in a meeting that you thought was for some other purpose. Have a valid reason for participating in a meeting. During the meeting, reach decisions and ensure that people leave with a clear understanding of the decisions. These suggestions also apply to a telephone conference call.

6. Identify snags in the workflow. Develop a time consciousness in your group by encouraging people to look for ways of streamlining procedures. A suggestion that saves 15 minutes a day adds up to a saving of 8 workdays per year.

7. Avoid the I-can-do-it-faster-myself syndrome. Many managers avoid delegation because they do not consider the time spent showing someone how to do a task as an investment. While delegation initially requires more time, it becomes a valuable time

investment when employees can assume recurring tasks.

If you are fortunate enough to have a secretary, make full use of this valuable resource. In addition to maintaining your calendar and managing a tickler file for follow-up, secretaries are ideal candidates for editing reports and doing research. The more your secretary understands about your job, the more you can effectively delegate.

8. Confront your procrastination. Most managers put things off that they don't like to do. If you specifically identify why you dislike the task, you may uncover the real reason for your procrastination. For example, if you do not know how or where to start a certain project, simply list in no particular order what you think needs to be done. It is then much easier to look at what you have written and assign a sequence. If you are procrastinating because you are overwhelmed by the size or complexity of the project, break it down into smaller tasks that can be worked into your daily schedule. If you are procrastinating until you have the perfect solution, be sure to weigh the risk of a missed opportunity against the risk of taking action before all the votes are in. By rolling up your sleeves and getting started, you are better prepared to deal with problems that may arise. By waiting until the last minute, you are extending an invitation to Murphy's Law.

9. Develop a plan for each day. Have you ever started your day with a to-do list of 15 items and ended the day with a to-do list of 22 items—including the original 15? This testifies to the fact that a manager's

day is filled with interruptions and spur-of-the-moment meetings. That's not to say that a to-do list isn't helpful. It is. When you review your list at the end of each day, evaluate what you have accomplished and how your time was spent. Then plan tomorrow's action items and anticipate any problems that might arise.

Also, try not to end each day with a to-do list that accounts for every waking minute and is impossible to complete. Instead, build into your schedule some disposable time for unplanned interaction. In this way, you are accessible to your people and have more time to build working relationships. Go home with a sense of accomplishment and avoid the demoralizing feeling that tomorrow you will be even further behind.

10. Do the most important thing now. Be aware of the significance of the task you are working on and make sure it represents the best use of your time as a manager. Once you recognize that your effectiveness is a function of what you do with your time as well as what you choose not to do, you can establish appropriate priorities and delegate more effectively. As a result, your group's performance will increase since you will have more time to devote to your most important job: managing.

Chapter 6:
What Do You Expect?

"Briggs, I told you not to expect much from Jones --- didn't I?"

"But no, you ignored my advice and gave him a more challenging assignment. And now look what's happened."

"But Mr. Adams --- Bob Jones has become my department's star performer."

"How could you do this to me, Briggs?"

Expectations play a major role in team member performance. This role is often referred to as the Pygmalion effect: a self-fulfilling prophecy in which people perform to the level of the expectations that are placed on them. Pygmalion is the original title of a play written by George Bernard Shaw which was renamed "My Fair Lady" for the Broadway musical. The story concerns two British associates who place a bet on whether a tattered, unsophisticated flower girl named Eliza Doolittle can be transformed into an eloquent, refined British lady. Eliza's most memorable line, which symbolizes the Pygmalion effect, is: "The difference between a lady and a flower girl is not how she behaves, but how she's treated."

Numerous studies have verifed this phenomenon in the classroom, business world and in the military. The studies randomly assigned individuals to high and low performer categories and gave the supervisors (or instructors) contrived ratings. Repeatedly, those individuals from whom supervisors expected better performance outperformed those designated as low performers.

These studies show that if people are treated like winners, they are more likely to succeed, and if treated as losers, are more likely to fail. Why? Designated winners concentrate on succeeding and capitalize on opportunities for success. Designated losers, on the other hand, are so worried about failing that they avoid situations with a risk of failure. However, since chances of success usually contain an element of risk, the losers end up avoiding the very situations that could turn them into winners.

A similar concept is suggested by the Wallenda factor, named after a famous tightrope aerialist, Karl Wallenda, who died from a fall in 1978. Unfortunately, prior to that fall, Karl became obsessed with a fear of falling and, for the first time, poured more energy into securing the high wire than into the actual walking of the tightrope.

For the manager, these are powerful examples because they suggest that performance can be affected by altering the expectation. If people are viewed in terms of what they can become rather than what they have been, the manager can positively influence individual and team accomplishments. The next time someone tells you not to expect much from an employee, try doing the opposite . . . you might just create a star.

While low expectations present a problem to team effectiveness, the reverse situation can also reduce performance. When expectations are unrealistically high, employees feel that the goals are unattainable. Therefore, expectations should be challenging but achievable.

A third problem is that of unclear expectations. People are not energized when goals are ambiguous. To increase productivity, people should clearly understand and agree to the expectations. Note the two key words in that sentence: understand and agree. To help people understand, clearly state what is expected. To help people agree, explain why it is expected. If people clearly understand but disagree with the expectations, the likelihood of accomplishment is significantly lower than if people had agreed to them. So how does a manager clarify expectations?

Management myth #6:

Expectations should only be discussed during formal performance appraisals.

Since formal performance appraisals focus on how well a person has met expectations, a communication of expectations *only* during an appraisal is like marking the finish line after someone has run the race. Unfortunately, it is usually by default that expectations are discussed during this forum. Unless people are forced to meet and discuss expectations, they rarely do so. The exception is that of the new employee who is given a job description. But even in this case, managers rarely seek up-front agreement to the job description by asking, "What are your thoughts on the expectations of this position?"

More importantly, expectation discussions should not be reserved for new employees. All employees need to know what is expected of them, both individually and as a team. In addition to frequent one-on-one discussions, it is also productive to hold group discussions on team expectations. You can begin a group meeting with a statement of the team's specific goals to ensure that everyone shares the same priorities and is pulling in the same direction. Then, by clarifying the role each team member plays, you can reduce duplication of effort as well as the likelihood of things "falling through the crack" (commonly known as the but-I-thought-you-were-doing-that syndrome). Such discussions instill a sense of ownership for the team goals and can be held once a month, once a quarter, or as often as needed.

Expectations are not a one-way proposition. We all bring expectations to our jobs—not only of what we should be doing, but expectations of what others should be doing as well. This means that the people you manage have expectations of how you should be doing your job. Since your role is to get things done through your people, consider asking them the following question: "As your manager, what can I do *more of* or *less of* to help you get the job done?"

Many managers are threatened by this approach because they fear criticism. Yet, this approach can significantly improve your ability to interact effectively with the individuals in your group. The "more of" suggestions should generate new ideas and the "less of" suggestions will raise your awareness of behaviors that inhibit people's performance. Managers are often unaware of the negative effects their actions are causing and, unfortunately, do not find out until a major crisis occurs.

This two-way approach, therefore, is a win-win situation: Your demonstrated willingness to meet your people's expectations will make them more likely to meet your expectations, thereby creating a cohesive team.

Finally, become expectation-focused in your daily communication with people. For example, how many times have you used the word "problem" without specifically defining what the problem was? The problem may be clear to you but not so to others. Vague phrases like "as soon as possible" and "find out what you can," or comments such as "the project is not running smoothly" and "we're not selling enough," lack clarity regarding expectations and leave room for individual interpretation and misunderstanding.

Specifically defined expectations increase the probability that requests and assignments will meet with execution. For example, give a specific date and time instead of "ASAP." Clarify a need to improve by stating how much of an improvement is expected. Make sure your team members can answer the question, "What do you expect?" with something other than shrugged shoulders.

Chapter 7:
Is Your Feedback Back-Firing?

"Crane, I'm really disappointed in your first week's results. All you have done is spend time with your people. You've let me down."

"It really upsets me to have to scold you like this. I can't tell you how depressed it makes me feel."

"How long have you been having this problem, Mr. Adams?"

". . . it all started in the third grade when the teacher. . . . . ."

Feedback lets employees know how well they are doing. But only effective feedback will improve performance. What's the difference? Effective feedback focuses on specific observable behavior, while ineffective feedback focuses on everything else.

First, effective feedback is specific. You can not reinforce positive actions and eliminate negative actions with vague comments. If you tell someone to "keep up the good work," what actions are you reinforcing? Or if you say, "I know you can do better," what actions are you eliminating?

Secondly, effective feedback focuses on behavior. Adjectives alone will not increase performance. For example, if you thank someone for being efficient and ambitious but fail to state the activity which prompted this compliment, you have not reinforced specific behavior. Or, if you tell someone, "Your performance lacks initiative," without stating the particular actions that are unacceptable, you have not given the employee a definite behavior to correct.

Thirdly, effective feedback focuses on behavior that is observable. Since attitudes can not be *seen*, any feedback dealing with a team member's attitude is judgmental or biased. Managers can only guess at someone's attitude, but they can see someone's behavior. Therefore, to improve performance, feedback should focus on what people have done rather than on what you think their attitude is.

Management myth #7:

The purpose of
feedback is to
make the manager
feel important.

This myth ignores the fact that advice-giving feedback can often be delivered at the expense of the employee's development. For example, many managers believe it is their responsibility to personally solve the problems of team members. As a result, when an employee complains about a situation, the automatic response is to tell the employee what to do. Instead, by asking, "How can we improve the situation?", the manager encourages employees to think for themselves. Similarly, when an employee complains about another employee, the typical management response is, "Let me talk to him/her," rather than asking the employee, "What are your ideas on how we can solve this problem?" The major difference between the two responses is that the latter contributes to employee development, which is the real purpose of effective feedback.

Encouraging employees to discuss their own progress represents another developmental opportunity for them. One of the best ways to stimulate this involvement is to communicate your own fallibility. When managers admit their mistakes and share what they have learned from them, others feel freer to do the same. Furthermore, these discussions should not be limited to formal appraisals. There are many opportunities in between appraisals to ask your people how they think they are performing.

The same is true of your feedback to employees. Effective feedback is timely and coincident with the employee's actions. If you accumulate compliments or let criticism fester until the performance review, you have significantly reduced your ability to maximize individual performance. So, be timely in delivering praise as well as suggestions for improvement.

Many managers feel uncomfortable discussing an employee's needs for improvement. To reduce the threat to yourself and the employee, there are specific steps to observe in correcting someone's behavior:

1. Clarify the expectation. The first step is to ask yourself whether the person clearly understands what is expected. If the answer is no, clarify the expectation and make sure the person understands what good performance means.

2. Clarify the capability. The second step is to ask yourself whether the person is capable of doing what is expected. Capability is the result of experience and training levels. Answering this question reduces the likelihood of criticizing employees for not doing something they are not trained to do.

3. Clarify the desired behavior. When performance is unacceptable and you can answer yes to the questions in Steps 1 and 2, the third step is to focus on the specific observable behavior. Prior to meeting with the employee, it is helpful to jot down the actual behavior that needs improvement; in this way, you can reference the employee's specific actions. Then, clarify the desired behavior (improve by how much and by when?) so that the employee knows exactly what to work on.

4. Schedule a meeting. Try to meet with the employee that same day, if possible. Rather than be mysterious about the purpose of the meeting, it is

better to mention the issue briefly and schedule a mutually agreeable meeting time. Those managers who meet with employees only when something is wrong will prompt a defensive reaction whether they mention the purpose of the meeting or not. But managers who regularly provide effective feedback can maintain an atmosphere of open communication and trust by mentioning the reason for the meeting.

5. Meet with the employee. Discussions of this nature should always be conducted in private. One approach for presenting this feedback is to mix praise with criticism by recognizing something the person is doing well before identifying the specific behavior that needs to be improved. This does not mean you should always say something positive before criticizing behavior. Overuse of this approach causes people to brace themselves whenever you praise them. But if this practice is used as a method of guidance and communication, reinforcing the employee's value as a total person, it can be very effective. The better people feel about themselves, the better they perform.

A second effective approach is to solicit employee participation in the discussion. For example, suppose that a team member makes a decision you disagree with. Rather than criticizing the person's business judgment, it is more helpful to determine the employee's reasons behind the decision. You might ask what alternatives the employee saw in making this decision. When you ask without being angry or critical, people are more apt to admit a mistake. On the other hand, you may discover that the employee

50

made the best decision based on the information available at that time. Therefore, your response might be a suggestion for better data gathering. Or it may even turn out that no criticism is warranted. Not only have you saved yourself an embarrassing moment, you have prevented a situation that could potentially erode your working relationship with the employee. Finally, if the discussion reveals that the employee's decision is incorrect, you can continue to keep the employee involved by asking, "What would have been a more effective decision?"

Both approaches make it easier for you and the employee to develop a mutually acceptable plan for improvement (which is the next step). If criticism is delivered by talking *at* the person, the employee leaves your office with resentment and a resistance to change. Instead, by mixing praise with criticism or by involving employees in their own feedback, you increase the likelihood of obtaining their agreement to improve.

6. Develop a plan for improvement. Once again, it is critical to involve the employee in identifying the specific actions necessary to achieve the desired behavior. In this way, you ensure that the employee understands *how* to improve. At the same time, it is important to display a sincere desire in helping the employee to do so.

7. Follow-up. By immediately recognizing signs of improvement, the manager reinforces the desired behavior and communicates to the employee that the company wants him/her to succeed.

If the manager has taken all these steps and the employee's behavior remains unchanged, the manager should discuss the consequences the individual faces if the behavior does not improve (ie. suspension, demotion, termination). Note that this is a last resort and the manager should continue to emphasize a willingness to help the employee correct the problem. In their book, *Discipline Without Punishment*, Richard C. Grote and Eric L. Harvey advocate "treating the employee as an adult with a problem to solve instead of a child who must be punished for misbehavior." As a final step in resolving persistent employee problems, the authors recommend a decision-making leave of one day with pay, during which the person must decide whether to change the behavior or resign to find more satisfying work elsewhere.[7] A day's leave with pay emphasizes the company's desire to help the employee solve the problem. In essence, this approach seeks increased employee commitment through coaching rather than punishment.

Feedback is a powerful management tool and, if used effectively, can dramatically increase team performance. Instead of being a source of discomfort and distress, why not make your feedback the pause that refreshes?

Chapter 8:
Are Rewards Merely
A Penny For Your
Thoughts?

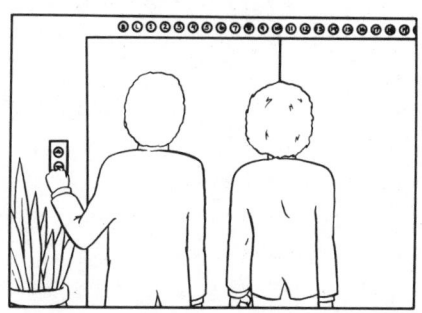

"I don't know, Susan. The quarterly bonuses just don't seem to have the same impact they once did. I mean,"

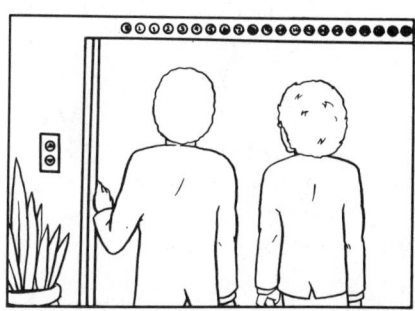

"cash is no longer the universal motivator. Today people have very specific ideas about what they consider a reward."

"What about you? How would you like to be rewarded for this job?"

"How about a year's supply of aspirin..."

Rewards can stimulate high levels of performance. Yet what comes to mind when you read the word "reward"?

Management myth #8:

*The only rewards
that have any
impact are
raises, bonuses
and promotions.*

Numerous surveys asking employees to rank the importance of motivational factors have revealed that wages and promotion opportunities are no longer the primary motivators for today's workers. Not that today's employees do not want good wages and promotions—they do. But the fact that they are better educated and self-directed makes them more motivated by factors such as challenging work, a sense of participation, and by the knowledge that their work is appreciated.

Frederick Herzberg, author of *Work and the Nature of Man*, used the term "hygiene factors" to identify aspects of a job which prevent dissatisfaction but do not produce motivation. He used the example of fringe benefits to illustrate that people are dissatisfied without benefits, but that a fringe benefit package does not, in itself, motivate performance. In the same manner, good wages alone are not enough to increase performance. Why? Employees eventually realize that they need only function at a certain level in their position to continue drawing the same wage. This does not mean that all employees will "coast"; but in the absence of meaningful motivators, where is the incentive for people to knock themselves out? As a result, compensation incentive plans were developed to increase performance.

Yet, bonuses are not the panacea. For example, when year-end bonus pools are distributed with the notion that every employee should receive something, the bonus becomes a disincentive for the high performers. Increasing the frequency of bonuses is no guarantee either, since companies are discovering that a $1000 quarterly bonus is not particularly motivational if it only serves to place the employee in a higher tax bracket. Nor does doubling the size of the bonus necessarily increase its motivational impact, due to a fundamental principle of motivation: People do things for their own reasons—not yours.

In other words, what is highly motivational to one person may provide absolutely no incentive to someone else. The dual career couple is often earning a comfortable joint income. Additional time off in this situation might provide more motivation than an extra $1000. Or consider the single parent with child care responsibility. This person might find motivation in flexible working hours but not in a trip to Hawaii. As a matter of fact, many companies who reward top performers with annual trips are finding themselves inundated with employee requests to trade the value of the trip for something else. Generally, these requests are denied and the companies end up losing the motivational impact the trip was designed to stimulate.

It is particularly interesting that organizations have recognized the obsolescence of one-size-fits-all in the area of employee benefit packages (originally designed for a male head-of-household with a wife who stayed home and cared for the children). Today, flexible benefit plans (flex plans) which allow employees to tailor their level of medical, life and disability insurance are widely available. Some plans even allow employees to buy additional vacation days after they have met certain minimum levels of coverage. When Comerica, a Michigan bank holding company, implemented a flex plan in 1983 called

"Custom Comp," over 90% of the employees elected to rearrange existing benefits.[8]

Even though these flex plans result in higher employee satisfaction and may influence a person's decision to work for a company, they do not increase performance since benefits are not viewed as something earned for a job well done. Yet, if people have very exact ideas about the types of insurance they want, it is reasonable to assume that they also have very specific ideas about how they want to be rewarded for outstanding performance. As a result, organizations are beginning to offer more customized forms of reward, such as sabbaticals, health club memberships and personal use of company resources. Why not increase performance by giving people what motivates them?

Promotion opportunity, like wages, is also not the paramount motivator for everyone. For many people, challenging work is more motivational than a potential promotion two years in the future. However, it is important to realize that a lack of promotion opportunity can be a demotivator; managers who selfishly hold back their employees are sacrificing long-term potential for short-term gain. When employees' careers are put on hold, resentment builds; they withdraw their support, and their performance either declines or disappears (through resignation). Instead, by acting as a career coach and informing employees how they can best prepare for promotion, you motivate employees through personal and professional development opportunities in their respective jobs. Then, as you promote the qualified employees who want to advance (not everyone wants to move up), the future successes of these employees reflect positively on you. For those employees who do not desire promotion, you can help them become the very best in their field. By being known as a manager who helps others realize their professional goals, good people will always be happy to work for you.

Another major distinction is the difference between recognition and reward. A reward is something given in return for achievement, while recognition is an expression of appreciation for achievement. The manager who thinks that reward and recognition are the same overlooks their combined potential for stimulating performance. For example, if an organization rewards twenty year service anniversaries with a gold pen set, and the manager merely places the set in an employee's mail slot rather than personally presenting it, the motivational impact is lost. The same is true for the manager who delivers a bonus check and basks in the employee's gratitude rather than saying to the person, "You earned this bonus and I appreciate your hard work. Thank you."

Appreciation is a powerful motivator and represents an unlimited commodity over which managers have total control. The same can rarely be said for bonuses, raises or promotions. Yet, appreciation is often the most under-utilized motivational tool. Why? One reason is that some managers are not aware of its capacity to stimulate performance. Another reason is that some managers do not feel they can take the time. Or, even worse, some managers never think of it.

What are some of the ways that you can harness the power of appreciation?

1. Recognize progress, not just end results. As a manager, your job is to increase team performance. But expressing appreciation only for the end result is like passively waiting until the game is over, instead of actively coaching while the game is in play. When a project milestone has been achieved, when a research breakthrough has occurred, or when two out of three competitors in a bid process have been eliminated, the manager should take advantage of this opportunity to motivate even higher levels of performance by praising the progress to date.

2. Be sincere. Genuine appreciation is relatively inexpensive. How much does it cost to say thank you or to send a letter of thanks to an employee? Send a note of thanks to a spouse for the long hours the employee has devoted to a project. Take an employee to lunch to express your appreciation. Buy a coffee mug for the secretary who typed the lengthy sales proposal. The value of appreciation lies more in the sincerity of the expression than in its price tag.

When a 1980 survey of workers at Diamond Fiber Products, manufacturer of paper egg cartons, revealed that 79% of the employees thought they were not being rewarded for a job well-done, management realized it was focusing its attention on the problem employees while ignoring the majority of the work force that was doing a good job. After instituting a program, known as The 100 Club™, that recognized employees for good attendance, safety and productivity, a subsequent survey reported that 81% of the workers felt their work was recognized.

The cost: $15,000 in nylon 100 Club jackets, dinners-for-two, hotel overnights and small appliances. The benefit: Diamond saved $1.6 million in the first year through dramatic decreases (40% or more) in absenteeism, injuries, quality-related mistakes and grievances as well as a 14% increase in efficiency. Why did this program succeed while similar programs at other companies are disparagingly referred to as "trash-and-trinket" programs by the employees? The difference lies in the sincerity of the appreciation. Diamond's management honestly communicated to the employees that the company was no longer going to take the workers for granted. Daniel C. Boyle, Vice President-Treasurer, states:

> We were careful not to position The 100 Club as a canned incentive program or just another management trick to get employees to work harder. Instead, we emphasized that The 100 Club is a way of demonstrating management's appreciation for the employees who allow Diamond to stay in business. It is not a financial incentive plan and it is more than a recognition program. It's a work style.[9]

Managers at Diamond treat workers as a vital part of the organization by sharing financial and competitive information. More importantly, managers solicit employee ideas and explain why workers are being asked to do things. For the employees, the value of the program is not in prizes but in the demonstration of genuine appreciation. For the company, the result of workers feeling valued has been a steady increase in productivity since The 100 Club began five years ago.

3. Help everyone feel like a winner. If a salesperson lands a major contract which qualifies her for a major reward that she values and a recognition luncheon, clearly she will feel like a winner. But what about the behind-the-scenes employees who contributed pieces to the success? Letters to these individuals (or to their managers) thanking them for their contribution, informs them that you appreciate their efforts. Not only does this stimulate performance, it also fosters greater cooperation in the future. Another win-win situation.

Effective use of reward and recognition profoundly increases performance; however, as with feedback, you must be timely. When a reward is presented according to a predetermined schedule, it may not coincide with the performance it is commending. When organizations let employee accomplishments stack up over a considerable period of time, the motivational impact of the reward is reduced. In many cases, a timely phone call from the vice president is far more meaningful and motivational than a plaque and a handshake received six months later. Remember, praise is like champagne—best served while it's still bubbling.

Chapter 9:
R-E-S-P-E-C-T: How Do You Spell Self-Esteem?

"I've called you here for a brainstorming session on the marketing strategy. Let's open our minds and do some free thinking. Remember, NO idea is too stupid."

"Mr. Adams, perhaps we should consider targeting a totally different market."

"That's ridiculous, Crane. You can't be serious."

". . . Now, who else has an idea to share?"

Self-esteem is an impression of self-worth. In the workplace, self-esteem includes the evaluation people have of their own ability and indicates the extent to which they believe themselves capable of making a contribution.

Management myth #9:

*Building self-esteem
is a parent's job—
not a manager's.*

Fortunately, this myth is diffusing due to individuals such as John Naisbitt and Patricia Aburdene who advocate "a new respect for the individual" in their book, *Re-inventing the Corporation*. Bill McGrane, founder of the Self-Esteem Institute, also emphasizes the value of high self-esteem in the workplace. Over 5000 professionals have attended McGrane's programs to learn how to raise employee self-esteem.[10] Despite this progress, however, there are still many managers who unintentionally make statements that demean employees. Regrettably, these managers are unaware of their negative impact on employee self-esteem.

For example, when a manager tells an employee, "You just don't seem to understand" or "I'm surprised to hear that from you," the manager is conveying a negative evaluation that the employee is inept or incompetent. The statement is received as a personal attack and can cause defensiveness, leaving the employee feeling demeaned. Problem-solving is then inhibited since the employee stops listening and/or cooperating.

Other examples of managerial statements that attack employee self-esteem are, "You should know better" and "I'm really disappointed in you." Instead of dealing with the behavior, these statements degrade the human being and leave the person with nothing specific to work on. The negative effect then snowballs since low self-esteem reduces participation which reduces performance.

On the other hand, when people feel good about themselves, they are more energetic, more productive and more committed. Therefore, you can positively affect employee self-esteem and increase team vitality by treating people with dignity and respect. Here's how:

1. Avoid statements that embarrass or demean employees. If this kind of statement slips out, apologize by stating, "I'm sorry, what I meant to say is . . ." Then focus on the issue—not the person. In this way, you will not damage the employee's self-esteem.

2. Respect your employees' time. Some managers think nothing of keeping their employees waiting for appointments or allowing interruptions during a meeting. However, if you treat people's time as the valuable commodity it truly is, you will enhance employee self-esteem.

3. Listen with full attention. When managers continue to take phone calls or read mail while an employee is talking with them, the manager implicitly communicates that the employee is less important. Instead, if the employee has come by at an inconvenient time, simply say, "I cannot give you my full attention right now. Can you meet with me at 3:00 this afternoon?" Ironically, managers think this may offend the employee, yet do not think twice about doing other things while the employee is talking. In scheduling to meet later that same day, you are letting employees know that what they have to say is important. Attentive listening is the best way to demonstrate respect.

4. Treat your employees as investments. Instead of adopting a short-term what-have-you-done-for-me-lately approach, demonstrate your willingness to invest in your people through training and development. Unfortunately, when managers view employee training as an expense rather than an investment, training classes are continually cancelled. And when managers narrowly define training as formal instruction, they typically hand employees over to the company training department. Yet there is no substitute for learning by doing and managers should encourage on-the-job training. If an active role is taken in an employee's ongoing development, high self-esteem is reinforced.

Delegation is another way of investing in your people since it encourages employees to accept responsibility and develop problem-solving skills. However, delegation should not be a form of dumping. Managers who delegate only boring or distasteful tasks demotivate their employees. Also, when responsibility is delegated without the commensurate authority, the employee's efforts are hampered by a lack of decision-making power. Instead, if you hand over both the responsibility for results and the authority for achieving them, you can upgrade employee decision-making skills and boost an individual's self-esteem. When you allow the employee to decide *how* to carry out a delegated task, you are demonstrating confidence in his/her ability. Then, by building in feedback mechanisms, such as periodic progress reports, you can offer guidance and stay apprised of the project's status without constantly peering over the employee's shoulders.

5. Recognize contributions. Recognition is an important ingredient in fostering team member self-esteem. As discussed in Chapter 8, employees need to know their performance is valued.

6. Share information. Pass on company information that affects your employees as soon as possible. This includes both good and bad news. Managers who pass on bad news and fail to include positive company results ignore the motivation potential of making everyone feel like a winner. The other extreme is also dangerous, since managers who withhold or sugar-coat bad news erode their people's trust. Expect a negative reaction if your employees learn information through the grapevine that they should have heard from you. Therefore, whenever possible, promote employee self-esteem by letting team members hear information from you before they hear it elsewhere. Also, workers become more committed to the business if you are willing to open the company books.

7. Focus on your team members. In today's me-oriented society, it is difficult not to talk about one's self. Try to carry on a conversation without using the words "I", "me" or "my," and notice the conscious effort this requires. Therefore, to secure cooperation from others, the manager must concentrate on the word "you" and remain more attentive to individual team members.

8. Demonstrate that employees have influence. The feeling of powerlessness at work drains employee self-esteem. When managers disregard employee suggestions or do not allow participation in decision-

making, self-esteem suffers and cooperation is replaced by in-fighting and finger-pointing. By contrast, if management solicits the points of view of employees and acts upon suggestions, self-esteem is significantly increased. The people who actually do the job know the most about how to improve it; when workers are allowed to carry out their own ideas, productivity is boosted.

9. Enhance the way your employees see themselves. Take away the fear of trying new approaches by regularly communicating confidence in their ability to succeed. This increases their level of commitment which means they will apply more energy to the job. With that energy comes more innovation and increased performance, vital to your long-term success as a manager.

Lastly, consciously work on your own self-esteem. Instead of focusing exclusively on mistakes, take time to recap the things you did well each day or during the past week. Then, rather than berating yourself with self-destructive criticism, identify what you have learned from your mistakes so you can continue to grow as a manager and a human being. It is difficult, if not impossible, to help others feel valued as individuals if you do not feel good about yourself.

Epilogue

"Briggs, Crane, I'm amazed at your results. Productivity and morale have sharply increased in your departments."

"I thought I knew every trick in the book. Tell me. . . how'd you do it?"

"Basically, Mr. Adams, we treat people like human beings."

"And they buy it?"

Management myth #10:

These techniques
will guarantee
your success.

While Susan Crane and David Briggs have learned numerous methods for increasing team performance, they know that a manager's ultimate success depends on an honest desire to earn people's trust and build employee commitment. Managers who use the latest gimmicks or tricks are undermined by insincerity; the words may be positive and enthusiastic, but the tone of voice, gestures and facial expressions expose the facade.

This book does not claim to be the only way of managing. It does suggest that in becoming more like a consultant to your workforce—a coach and coordinator who is willing to share, to listen, to ask (rather than tell), to teach and to counsel—employees will produce. Here lies the difference between a boss and an effective manager.

APPENDIX

There are several factors to consider in selecting a self-assessment instrument (Chapter 2):

1) Is the instrument reliable and valid? The goal of self-understanding is to obtain objective information about yourself. Make sure the questionnaire has been statistically validated as a reliable, unbiased indicator of behavioral traits; otherwise, you might receive incorrect information about your behavior. Inquire about the validity of the instrument, including research, populations sampled and published studies endorsing the instrument's reliability.

2) Is the instrument professionally administered? Administration of the questionnaire by a certified professional provides the optimum setting for taking the instrument. More importantly, it ensures an accurate interpretation of the questionnaire results.

3) Does the instrument deal specifically with the way you interact with others? For the purpose of enhancing management effectiveness, it is essential that the instrument focus on interpersonal behavior. Otherwise, the information may not directly apply to your role in managing others.

One instrument that meets all the criteria is the Personal Profile System distributed by Performax Systems International, Inc., 12755 State Highway 55, Minneapolis, Minnesota, 55441, (612) 559-2322.

SELECTED REFERENCES

[1] From a filmed interview with Bear Bryant by Dr. John Geier, "Nothin' But A Winner," distributed by Performax Systems International, Inc., 1982.

[2] *Attitudinal Listening Profile System Manual*, Performax Systems International, Inc., 1982.

[3] ibid

[4] ibid

[5] Printed with permission from Jeffrey Kreis, owner of Walnut Creek Train Station, Walnut Creek, California.

[6] Fitzpatrick, Jean Grasso, "Stop Working Late," Working Woman, October 1983.

[7] Printed with permission from Eric L. Harvey, Performance Systems Corporation, Dallas, Texas.

[8] Tane, Lance D. and Treacy, Michael E., "Benefits That Bend With Employees' Needs," Nation's Business, April 1984.

[9] Printed with permission from Daniel C. Boyle, Diamond Fiber Products, Inc., Thorndike, Massachusetts.

[10] Printed with permission from Bill McGrane, McGrane Self-Esteem Institute, Cincinnati, Ohio.

READER'S NOTES

READER'S NOTES

READER'S NOTES